Picture Composition; Primary Level, Std-I to V

Development of Writing Skills from Single Sentence Formation to Paragraph Writing (including question patterns & answer guide)

Mr. Peter

DEDICATION

Dedicated to all the beloved children who are unique in their simplicity of mind, honesty, and lack of prejudice, the elders tend to impose upon a blank page.

BOOK SUMMARY

Mr. Peter's "Picture Composition: Primary Level, Std-I to V" is a key resource for developing writing skills from Primary to Secondary Level. This comprehensive guide effectively walks students through various writing styles, transitioning from basic sentence construction to mastering Paragraph and Picture Story Composition.

The curriculum is organized in clear stages, progressing from simple sentences to more complex structures, culminating in well-crafted short paragraphs based on visual prompts. Initially, students receive ample support through prompts and examples, which are gradually reduced as they advance. This thoughtful approach encourages critical thinking and empowers them to express their ideas independently while engaging with images.

In addition, the material encompasses a variety of unseen passages specifically designed to enhance Reading Comprehension skills. These passages provide opportunities for readers to engage with diverse texts, fostering critical thinking and analytical abilities. Furthermore, the study of English Grammar is intricately woven into the reading exercises, allowing learners to improve their grammatical knowledge while simultaneously honing their reading skills. This integrated approach not only supports language acquisition but also encourages a deeper understanding of how grammar functions within different contexts.

CONTENTS

<u>Introducing...</u>

In Picture Composition, the learner is presented with one or more pictures and is tasked with developing them into a story or writing a few lines or a paragraph based on the visual prompts.

Guidelines for Writing Good Picture Composition:

1. **Observe the Picture**: Take a moment to look at the details in the picture. Identify the principal elements and any subtle features that may be significant to the narrative.

2. **Note Down Observations**: Jot down points about what you see in each picture section. This could involve noting specific characters, objects, actions, and emotions.

3. **Ask Relevant Questions**: Formulate questions based on your observations. Consider what or who is present, what is happening, what activities are taking place, and how the characters might feel.

4. **Craft Your Paragraph**: Using the answers to your questions, start writing your paragraph. Ensure you connect the points logically to create a cohesive narrative that brings the picture to life.

By following these steps, you can create a well-structured and imaginative composition that captures the essence of the picture.

PICTURE STORY COMPOSITION (PRIMARY LEVEL)

STEP-1 (Single to Double Sentence Writing)

A. Beginner's Single Sentences: (suitable for standard-1)

Complete the sentences based on the pictures given:

This is a _________. (book)
That is a _________. (ball)

She is my .... (mom)
He is my _____________. (dad)

The girl is my _________. (sister)
The boy is my _________. (brother)

The girl is .... (talking over the phone)
The man is ____________________. (reading a book.)

The girls are .... (talking)

The boys are ____________________music. (playing)

The birds are ____________________ in the sky.
(flying)

The wolves are ...._. (howling)

The dog is _________________________________.

The boy is _________________________________.

B. Single Sentence Writing with Options: (Primary Level, Standard 1 to 5)

Complete the sentences based on options given in pictures (by using naming, describing, or doing words as necessary.)

The baby birds are feeling _____________ because _________
____

Answer guide:
a) happy, their parents are returning.
b) happy, the mother bird is feeding them.
c) excited, the day is breaking.

I would like to see ___________ because ___________________

____

Answer guide:

a) *cartoons, these are entertaining.*

b) *football match, it is thrilling.*

c) *news, it enriches my knowledge of the world.*

For a picnic, I like to go ___________ because ___________

____

Answer guide:

a) *on a beach, I love sunsets over the seas.*
b) *a zoo, I learn about different animals and birds as well.*
c) *hills, because seeing the sunrise over the peaks is cool.*

= _______________ is my favorite season because _______________

Answer guide:

a) *Rainy season, it is refreshing, and nature grows green around.*
b) *Winter season, ice falls around, and I love skating.*
c) *Spring, nature becomes colorful all around, and we can see different flowers in our garden.*

If I had a pet, I would ....

Answer guide:

    a) play with it.

    b) bathe it every day.

    c) watch TV sitting beside it.

C. Two or More sentences with examples (Primary Level, Standard 1 To 5)

Read the sentences about the picture on the left. Then, write two or more sentences for each about the pictures, given next:

Table-1

Maizie is going to school.
She walks to school every day.

Write two or more sentences against the picture.
1. ____________________________________
2. ____________________________________

Anna is riding a cycle. (write more two sentences)
1. ____________________________________
2. ____________________________________

Table-2

Pizza is a junk food. We should not ___________.
We should not eat it everyday.

Write two or more sentences against the picture.
1. _______________________________________
2. _______________________________________

There are fruits. (write more two sentences)
1. _______________________________________
2. _______________________________________

Table-3

Archie is a careless boy. One day, he threw ____ .
A man _______________________________________.

1. _______________________________________
2. _______________________________________

1. _______________________________________
2. _______________________________________

Table-4

Elias likes to draw paint. He just finished
__________.

It is about _________________________ .

Write two sentences against the picture

1. _______________________________

2. _______________________________

Leon sits before a piano. (write two more)

1. _______________________________

2. _______________________________

Table-5

Sonny is swimming in a river.

Swimming is good for health.

1. _______________________________

2. _______________________________

1. _______________________________

2. _______________________________

Answer Guide

Answer guide of the above tables (students' answers may vary, and that should always be welcomed):

1.

(a) I wash my hands daily before and after my meal. I use hand washing to wash my hands. It is hygienic for health.

(b) Anna loves cycling every day. She is going to her friend Alisha.

2.

(a) Pizza is junk food. We should not eat it every day, as it is harmful to our health.

(b) Milk is a healthy drink. Ember drinks two glasses of milk every day.

(c) Anna loves fruits. However, cherries are her favorite.

3.

(a) Archie is a careless boy. One day, he threw a banana peel on the road. A man stepped on it. He slipped and fell.

(b) Tom is a nice guy. He collects used bottles every Friday to keep his locality clean.

(c) Alisha is a good girl. She is helping her mother with her cooking.

4.

(a) Elias likes to draw paint. He just finished his paintings. It is about a tree and green grass beside a village.

(b) Little Dean likes his dolls. He fell asleep while he was playing with his dolls on the lawn.

(c) Leon is now in a music class. He is playing the piano on a popular song.

5.

(a) Elias is running with a football. He is pretty good at playing football. He wants to be an international player one day.

(b) Anna is a good girl. She is now doing her homework. After that, she likes to read a story of fairy tales.

STEP-2 (Writing Three or More Sentences, Using Clues)

D. Writing a short paragraph in three or more sentences (Primary Level, Standard 2 to 5)

Write three or more sentences _using the clues_ given based on the pictures. *(However, regarding points or clues, a learner is free to use his or her own.)*

Table-1

best friends, do everything together, different hobbies
- Finn & John are two best friends.
- They read & play together.
- However, they have different hobbies.
- Finn likes swimming, when John likes to play bad-minton.

Green plants, yellow carrot, important source of vitamins and minerals. good for eyes and skin.
- _______________________________________
- _______________________________________
- _______________________________________

colourful umbrella, looks attractive, protects from heat and rain.
- _______________________________________
- _______________________________________
- _______________________________________

Table-2

sick, resting in bed, did not go to school for three days.

- ____
- ____
- ____

horse cart, farmer taking hay, going to sell in the market.

- ____
- ____
- ____

green bus, traveling together, great fun

- ____
- ____
- ____

Table-3

father's office bag, grey, black zips, carrying documents and paper in it

- ____
- ____
- ____

a red boat, floating on a river, carries passengers and goods, used for short distances.

- ____
- ____
- ____

tortoise, happy, hard shell, walks slow, lives longer than human.

- ____
- ____
- ____

Table-4

deer, lives on grass, lives in forest, runs very fast.

- _______________________________________
- _______________________________________
- _______________________________________

pet dogs, different in color, different species in the world, layal and faithfull animal among all.

- _______________________________________
- _______________________________________
- _______________________________________

horse, four strong legs, beautiful crest upon the neck, many love horse riding.

- _______________________________________
- _______________________________________
- _______________________________________

Table-5

my father, my best friend, love father, takes care.

- _______________________________________
- _______________________________________
- _______________________________________

good friends like stars, do many things together, support us when we are sad.

- _______________________________________
- _______________________________________
- _______________________________________

wake up at 5 a.m., brush teeth, study till 9 a.m., getting ready for school, a daily routine

- _______________________________________
- _______________________________________
- _______________________________________

Table - 6

honeybee, collect nectar from flowers and store in hundred rooms, called honeycomb.
- _______________________________
- _______________________________
- _______________________________

Felix, a god boy, helps father, cleaning house & others.
- _______________________________
- _______________________________
- _______________________________

Leon, a good boy, loves study, has learnt many things, won competitions.
- _______________________________
- _______________________________
- _______________________________

Answer Guide to

best friends—carrots—umbrella—when you are sick—horse cart—green bus—father's office bag—boat on a river—tortoise—deer—pet dog—horse—about your father—good friends—daily routine—honey bee & honeycomb—cleaning your house & its surrounding—when you love your study;

Answer guides are only for assistance and giving learners information. Encourage your kids to write as many sentences as they can using the points or points thought by them or themselves to develop their writing skills. (Students' answers may vary, and that should be welcomed):

(1)

   a) Finn and John are best friends. They read and play together. However, they have different hobbies. Finn likes swimming, while John likes to play badminton.

   b) Carrots are yellow in color, but their plants are green like others. Carrot is an essential source of vitamins and minerals.

One who drinks half a cup of carrot juice daily hardly suffers from eye and skin disease.

c) Jacob has an umbrella. It is not colorful like Alisha's. An umbrella is a very useful instrument when it rains. It protects us from the sun's scorching heat in summer and rain in the rainy season.

(2)

(a) Sabine is a little girl. She has been sick for a few days. The doctor has asked her to take bed rest. She is resting in her bed. She did not go to school today.

(b) A horse cart is a horse-drawn vehicle. It is pulled by one or a team of horses. It is widely used in villages or countryside. A farmer uses a horse cart to take hay or sacks of corn from one place to another. A horse cart is going to market to sell corn.

(c) The Bus is a common means of transport on land. We travel on a bus to school every day, and many of my classmates also travel on this bus. We have so much fun traveling together. I love the song "Wheels on the Bus." It was green.

(3)

(a) This is a picture of my father's grey office bag. It has many black zips and pockets, where he carries his important documents and papers.

(b) There is a red boat on the river. A boat effortlessly floats on water. Many boats have engines. However, many others move on oars. Boats carry passengers and goods to reach them for a short distance.

(c) Tortoises belong to reptiles. It has hard shells. The hard shell protects it from outward threats. Tortoises can vary in size. Some swim best, others generally walk. They walk very slowly, and they always look happy. A tortoise lives longer than animals around us and even longer than human beings.

(4)

(a) Deer are mammals like cows, elephants, and humans. They live on green grass and in jungles. A male deer is called a **buck,** and a female deer is called a **doe**. However, some larger males are called **stags,** and female deer are called **hinds.** A young deer is called a **fawn**. Deer can jump up to 10 feet high, and they are excellent swimmers, too, and they are good runners on grass or land.

More about Deer:

(Deer is the only group of animals in the world with antlers. Antlers are the fastest-growing living tissue in the world! Each year, antlers fall off and regrow. There are over 60 different species of deer worldwide. Deer is present on all continents except Antarctica. All species of deer have antlers, with few exceptions, like the Chinese water deer.)

(b) Dogs are faithful and loyal animals. They become pets too quickly. There are different species of dogs worldwide, and they are of various sizes and colors. The sense of smell of a dog is at least 40x better than ours. Some dogs are incredible swimmers who can run very fast on land. Dogs have fewer holes in their skin, so they don't sweat like humans.

(c) A horse is a domesticated animal like a cow or goat. A horse is an odd-toed and hooped mammal. A horse has four strong legs, and they can run very fast. Horses are brilliant animals. And it is an animal that can sleep standing up. A male horse has 40 teeth, while a mare (a female horse) has only 36. Another essential fact about horses is that they can't breathe through the mouth like us, except through the nose. Horses are used for riding and transport. Some people have also kept horses as their pets since earlier days.

(5)

(a) Parents, a father and mother, are the most loving and caring persons in a family. Every mother and father cares for his or her child dearly and to the best of their capacity. However, I love my father most. He is the most dutiful person. He meets all my demands and takes care of my studies. I believe him to be an intelligent person too. He gives answers to all my questions as well. He is my best friend, guide, and philosopher. I love my father very much.

(b) Friends are the other name of love and trust. I am lucky that I have friends. Pitt and Tom are my best friends. We play together and often share our Tiffin. They are my stars. When I feel sad, they visit me, and I feel happy once again playing with them.

(c) I am Shreya. I read in class 2. I am an early riser. I wake up at 5 a.m. every morning and walk with my father for half an hour after brushing my teeth and washing my face. From 7 to 9 a.m., I study and then prepare for school, starting at 10 a.m. This is my daily routine from Monday to Friday. On Saturday and Sunday, I have a lot of fun. Sometimes, I also play video games.

(6)

(a) Honey bees belong to the family of insects. Honey bees are small insects. They are little yellow and black insects with wings and sharp stings, which we always fear! Generally, honey bees live in grasslands, forests, and gardens. However, recently, they have reared for economic importance. Honey bees collect nectar from flowers. From nectar, honey bees make honey and store that in hundreds of beehives. When the beehives are filled with honey, we call it a honeycomb. Men collect honey for their use from these honeycombs. It is of great economic importance to the human world.

(b) Felix is a good boy. He reads in class 2. However, he often helps his father clean the house and its surroundings. Felix and his family know well, that the best way of living healthy is to live in a clean home. Cleaning floors, kitchen, bathroom, and many others regularly eliminates germs, dirt, and dust and protects us from falling sick. We do not suffer from allergies and infections. Besides, housecleaning improves one's confidence levels and self-esteem, which also helps to acquire respect from others.

(c) Leon is a good boy. He loves to study very much. This habit of Lean led him to learn many things beyond his school syllabus. Besides, securing good marks in his examinations, Leon has participated in many competitions and has won medals.

STEP-3 (Writing Short Paragraphs, Using Clues)

E. Write short paragraphs against the pictures given, in 60 words only. You may use the clues shown in the first line. However, you are free to use your own:

Table-1

Ship: *white color, goes on seas and oceans, travel long distances)*
I can see a ship with white sails in the picture. A ship is a large watercraft that travels long distances on seas and oceans, as opposed to a boat which is a smaller watercraft to travel short distances in river. A ship carries passengers as well as cargos from one country to another. In earlier time, ships mainly floated on using sails and paddles. However, in modern time it floats and moves on engine.

The sun: rise in the east--warmth pleasant--a star--gives energy

____

____

____

____

Table-2

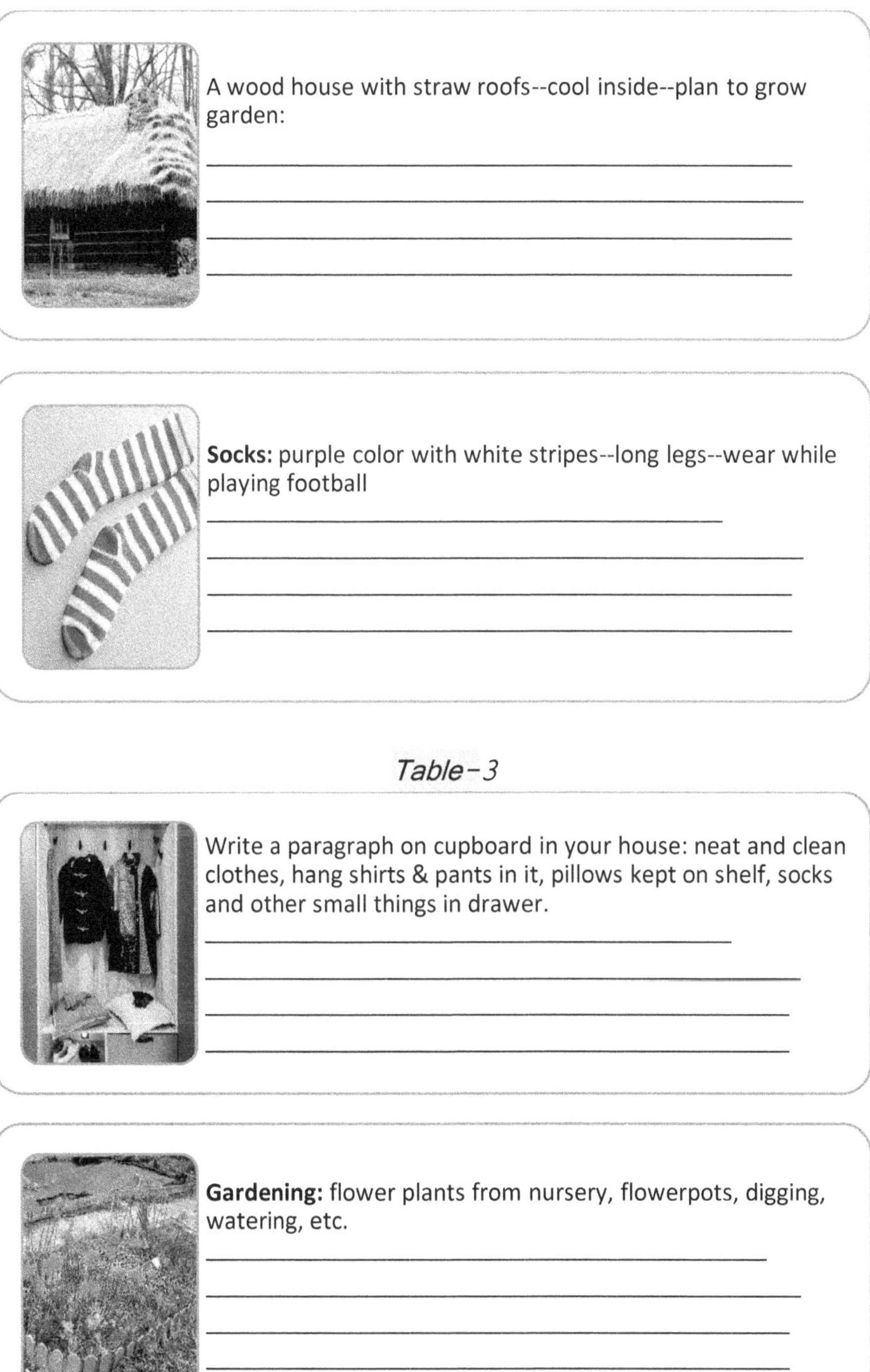

A wood house with straw roofs--cool inside--plan to grow garden:

____

____

____

____

Socks: purple color with white stripes--long legs--wear while playing football

____

____

____

____

Table-3

Write a paragraph on cupboard in your house: neat and clean clothes, hang shirts & pants in it, pillows kept on shelf, socks and other small things in drawer.

____

____

____

____

Gardening: flower plants from nursery, flowerpots, digging, watering, etc.

____

____

____

____

Table-4

Divya practices archery daily--exercises to stay fit--good aim--wants to go for Olympics one day

____

____

____

____

John is ambitious to be a great basket ball player:

____

____

____

____

Table-5

Little Sumi likes to read stories:buy books and colect from library too, sometimes exchange books with her friends.

____

____

____

____

Write a paragraph on your parents: (loving, caring, supporting, mention their profession, etc.

____

____

____

____

Table-6

Playing Chess: 8*8 square board with 16 pieces for each, have different styles of movement, an internationally played indoor game, develop persistence, patience & concentration

____
____
____
____

Peacock: largest & heaviset bird with a crown on head & dazzling colorful feathers, national bird in India

____
____
____
____

Table-7

Cooking: an art, need for healthy life, everyone should learn

____
____
____
____

Washing Clothes: bucket, water, detergent, dip clothes, scrub, rinse & dry

____
____
____
____

Answer Guide to

Ships—the Sun—wood house—socks—a cupboard in your house—gardening—Archery as your hobby—Playing basketball—reading story books—your parents—playing chess—peacock—cooking—washing clothes.

(Encourage your kids to innovate her or his own clues, and let her or him write as many sentences as far as s/he can. **That is good to develop his or her writing skills without restrictions.** The answer guide is provided only to add information and to help the student):

(1)

（b）We get up early every day when the sun rises in the east. The sun glows in the east sky with a yellow color, and its warmth is so pleasant and uplifting. The sun is a star in the center of the solar system. We are alive because of the sun. It gives us light, heat, and energy to move and work. The food that we consume is produced in the presence of sunlight. If there is no sun, no animal exists on the planet.

(2)

（a）Anita is **my best friend.** She lives in a house made of wood with a straw roof. It is cool inside. Anita and her parents love to grow a garden in front of their house. I helped them with baby flower plants from my parents' nursery. I love to visit Anita's house often and play together for hours.

（b）These are my **new pair of socks**, which my mother bought for me yesterday. They are purple with white stripes and do not have a shade like my earlier ones. They also have long legs. I like to wear them when I play football, and I wear a white pair when I go to school every day.

(3)

（a）You can see my **cupboard** here. There, I keep only my neat and clean clothes. My shirts and pants hang on hangers. Two pillows are also kept on the shelf. Small things, like socks, hand gloves, and ties, are neatly folded and kept in the drawers.

（b）**Gardening is growing and cultivating plants**, sometimes as a hobby and often as an economic activity to gain profits.

Peter likes gardening. He has a garden in front of his house. He collects flower plants from a local nursery. He uses some brown or colored pots. However, Peter prefers to plant them more on open ground than in small pots. He digs and adds some natural fertilizers before planting a plant. Peter's children water them every day when it is not the rainy season.

(4)

(a) **Divya** is a little girl in class VII. She **likes archery very much**. She practices it every day and also takes exercise to keep fit. Divya has a good aim in her archery. She has already won many school prizes and two medals at the district level. Divya wants to play in the Olympics one day.

(b) **Basketball is a great way to exercise and have fun with friends.** I started playing basketball when I was a kid. Now, I am a class VII student and play basketball for my school team. We have already won a few prizes since last year. Playing basketball requires a ton of stamina and a vast amount of energy, like playing football. It is an exercise. It keeps us fit and healthy. Like any other outdoor game, this game can bring us joy and foster better friendships among players.

(5)

(a) **Little Sumi likes to read stories** very much. For this, her father has bought her many storybooks from shopkeepers. Little Sumi also collects some books from the library in her locality. Her friends also like to read stories. Little Sumi often exchanges books with them.

(b) **My parents** are my strength to move on. I read in class V, and I love them very much. Perhaps there is no child who does not love his or her parents. They support us in more ways than we can count. My father is a schoolteacher, and he helps me with my studies. My mother is a doctor, and I have learned patience from my mom. My parents have two kids, I am, and my little sister, Edith.

(6)

(a) Different games help us to develop different aptitudes and skills. **Chess** is an internationally played game in the category of indoor games. The play of chess develops persistence, patience, and concentration. Chess is an 8 x 8 square board game played between two players. The chess consists of 2 sets of colored pieces, white and black. Each set has 16 pieces: precisely 8 pawns, 2 bishops, 2 knights, 2 rooks, 1 queen, and 1 king. Different types of pieces have different styles of movement. Pawns have the least power, while the queen holds the maximum power. I love playing chess. My father was my first master. I learned to play chess from him. It can also be played on a computer or mobile nowadays. However, I like to play it with my friends.

(b) **Peacock** is the largest and heaviest bird that can fly, though not so high in the sky. It has a small mouth and a vast body. The weight of the **peacock** is about 5 to 10 kg. A peacock has a crown and a long, gleaming dark blue neck. It has gorgeous feathers in a variety of colors. When it dances in the rain, spreading its all-feathers round, rippling, and its beauty instantly brings comfort to our eyes. For its magnificent beauty and significant religious involvement in Bharatiya traditions, the bird is considered the National Bird of Bharat.

(7)

(a) **Cooking** is an art that everybody should learn. Without cooked food, a human being can't live a healthy life. Cooking is required to make the food items edible and tasty, making us happy and healthy. I do cook, for I love having food. However, I can't do cooking as good as my mother does. But I can say my cooking is good enough to invite my friends often and have a lot of fun with them.

(b) We need to **wash our clothes** every day. It keeps us fit and healthy, and we can avoid many diseases using clean clothes. However, washing clothes includes the following steps.

- Step 1: Take a bucket and fill it with water;
- Step 2: Add Detergent, mix well, and dip your dirty clothes into the water;
- Step 3: leave for twenty to thirty minutes;
- Step 4: Scrubbed thoroughly one by one, and wash the clothes in fresh and clean water twice;
- Step 5: Rinse and dry;
- Step 6: Press and fold your clothes properly;
- Step 7: They are now ready to be used again.

STEP-4 (Writing Paragraphs, Without Clues)

（1） Look at the picture and write a few sentences for it:

A Picture of a Garden

This is a picture of a garden.
There are many flowers in the garden.

A butterfly is near the flowers.

There is a big tree. A bird is sitting on it.

(2) Carefully read another series of pictures given. Write short paragraphs observing the pictures:

A Park

Important points to remember: Think about the different parts of the pictures given. Think properly and express them in sentences. Read one example:

park   butterfly

rabbits   birds

Try to give answers to the questions:
- What is the album about? Is this about a park, garden, forest, or any other?
- What can be seen in different frames? Think of them in one place.
- Are there any birds, animals, men, or butterflies?
- Are there any flowers in the picture? And of what color?
- Try to recognize anything beyond these.

If we write the answers and arrange them properly:

This scene depicts a park filled with birds, flowers, butterflies, rabbits, and guinea pigs. Many long and large trees can also be found in this area. The park is vibrant, with various species of birds, rabbits, and flowers of different colors, all captured in other frames of an album. Some birds are perched high in the trees, while clusters of colorful flowers hang from the branches. On the ground, rabbits are seen gathering food or playing together. An orange and black butterfly is resting on some buds, adding to the park's beauty.

Mother Birds

(3) Look at the picture carefully and write seven sentences about it.

Mother birds always love their babies unconditionally. They spend much time caring for their babies and keeping them safe. Baby birds always depend on their parents to eat food. In this case, a mother bird usually digests the food and then puts that food into the baby's mouth. The babies always open their mouths wide and screech for food when hungry. The mother birds often feed their babies insects so that they can get more protein and grow healthy.

Birthday Party

（4） **Look at the picture carefully, and try to point out things to write about them in simple sentences.**

Every year I celebrate my birthday on 30th July and my elder brother celebrates his on 2nd December. However, this picture is my cousin's Lucy. We reached there in time. We wished her saying in rhythm and jointly 'Happy Birth Day to You,' "Many, Many Returns of the Day,' etc. We recited some other verses too together. Lucy served us a delicious cake, which her aunt had baked, and her mother had prepared mouth-watering dishes for all of us who attended the party that day. We celebrated the party with great joy and excitement together.

However, you may begin with: I am Lucy. I am five years old. Last Monday, I celebrated my....

Classroom

(5) Look at the picture carefully and write seven sentences about it.

My classroom is full of happy memories. We study there and play together after each period. Though our classroom is small, we love it dearly. Our classroom has several desks, a chair, and a table for our teacher. The teachers love us and take care of us. During Tiffin time, we have our Tiffin, but the best thing is playing together in the playground.

Flying Kite

(6) Look at the given pictures. Write three short paragraphs about what you think may have happened. Remember to write a title to your paragraphs.

Raju woke up early. It was a clear, sunny day, a perfect day to fly his kite, so he went to a nearby park with his kite.

The wind was favorable, and his kite went high in the sky. Raju was feeling excited.
Slowly, a strong breeze blew his kite towards a tall tree, and it got stuck in the branches. Raju tried hard to get his kite out of the tree but could not. He had no more kites to fly. Raju was sad. He had now no kite to fly. Raju returned home.

Good Habits

(7) The pictures below show some good habits every child must learn. **Write a short paragraph on good habits** with the help of the visual stimulus given below.

It is often said that "early to bed and early to rise makes a man healthy, wealthy, and wise." Developing good habits, like going to bed early, brushing our teeth, and taking morning walks, helps maintain cleanliness and fitness.

As social beings, we need interactions with others. It is important to respect elders and greet people politely. Helping those in need and following rules, like standing in a line, also help to create a better society.

Education focuses on building good character. We should study. In the end, good habits lead to good manners. Good manners help us form solid friendships and create a positive environment contributing to a happy and peaceful society.

STEP-5 (Writing Long Paragraphs, Observing Pictures)

Picture Description of a Magician

(1) Look at the Comic Picture and write a paragraph in about 100 words.

A Magician

Last Saturday, a magician visited our school. He was none but our Gafur Mia from the neighboring village. He took a white handkerchief from Ruma. He put it into his long brown cap on a wooden tool. Gili, Gili, Gili... choo-mantar, he made a round his magic stick over the cap, and the white handkerchief turned into a white cat. Mew, MEOUW!

Our teacher said, 'Magic is nothing but tricks and science.' Whatever it would be, it was a day of great fun for all the students to see the tricks or magic of Gafur Mia. (96 words)

Traffic Signals

(2) Suppose, one day, you were going to school on a walk along a road, and you saw an accident happen. Now, read the traffic rules carefully in succeeding posters and write a paragraph on **'Traffic Signals.'** Mention the causes of the accident and state some means to avoid such a tragic occurrence.

Causes: Breaking traffic rules, fast driving, animals on roads, Cyclists moving on the wrong lane.

Safety Rules: Follow traffic light signals, maintain the speed limit, and avoid using music or mobile phones while driving.

How to cross the road

- Hold your mother's or your dad's hand tight.

- Find a safe place to cross.

- Stop at the road sign.

- Think carefully.

- Look left.

- Look right and all around you.

- Listen to the horns of the cars, if any is coming.

- Cross safely and remember these rules.

Accidents are Tragic

____

____

____

____

_____________________________________ .

(3) Carefully read the points given below, and write a paragraph using them:

（a hungry dog—in search of food—got a piece of bone from a butcher's shop—crossed a bridge over the narrow river—and found another dog with a bone underwater—barked and lost his piece too in the water.）

Greedy Dog

Once there lived a dog. He was starving. He wandered here and there in search of food. He got a juicy bone from a butcher's shop. He felt very happy. He took the bone and ran away. He reached on a river bridge. He saw his own shadow in the water. He thought another dog had a juicy bone in his mouth. His mouth watered, and he wanted to snatch that bone from him. He started barking at him, and the bone fell into the water. He lost his own.

Moral: "Greed brings one closer to death."

(4) **See the picture. Has any idea come to mind? Now, study the points given and develop them into a story. (However, the story has been extracted from Aesop's Fables):**

The Hare and the Tortoise

Once, a tortoise and a hare were friends. The tortoise was slow, while the hare was fast and often teased him. One day, the tortoise challenged the hare to a race, and the hare agreed. The race began, and the hare quickly pulled ahead. Seeing a large tree by a lake, he took a nap, thinking he had plenty of time. Meanwhile, the tortoise steadily continued and soon reached the sleeping hare. He quietly passed him and nearly reached the finish line. When the hare woke up, he sprinted, but it was too late. The slow but steady tortoise crossed the finish line first, winning the race. (107 words)

Moral: 'Slow but Steady wins a race.

(5) **Read the picture series carefully and develop them into a story. Write a moral to it.**

The Mongoose and the Brahmin's Wife

A Brahmin lived with his wife and newborn son in a small village, along with their pet mongoose. One day, the Brahmin went to work while his wife went to fetch water, leaving the mongoose to watch over their child.

While they were gone, a cobra entered the house and approached the baby. The mongoose sensed the danger, attacked and killed the snake.

When the wife returned, she saw the mongoose with blood on its mouth and, assuming it harmed her son, killed it in anger. Entering the house, upon discovering her son safe and the dead snake nearby, she realized her terrible mistake: the mongoose had actually saved her child from the cobra.

Moral Lesson: Pause and Think Before Acting / Do not act hastily without understanding the situation.

(6) **Read the picture and the following points and develop them into a story. Write a moral to it.**

Four Friends and a Hunter

A deer, a turtle, a crow, and a rat were friends. They lived happily in a jungle. One day, the deer was caught in a hunter's trap, and the friends made a plan to save him. The deer struggled as if it was in pain, and then it lay motionless, with eyes wide open, as if it were dead. The crow and the other birds then sat on the deer and started poking it as they did to a dead animal. Right then, the turtle crossed the hunter's path to distract him. The hunter left the deer, assuming it dead, and went after the turtle. Meanwhile, the rat chew opens the net to free the deer while the crow picks up the turtle and quickly takes it away from the hunter.

Moral: Teamwork can achieve great results.

READING COMPREHENSION: UNSEEN PASSAGES

Reading Comprehension: Prose

(1) Read the picture story:

Ria has a new bicycle. It is bright pink and shiny and was a gift from her uncle. He hid it behind a bush to surprise her. Ria jumped joyfully when she saw the bicycle behind the bush.

She gave her uncle a big hug. She loves her new bicycle, and she loves her uncle.

A. Answer the following questions.

1. What is the color of the bicycle?
2. Who was it a gift from?
3. Where was it hidden?
4. What did Ria do when she saw the bicycle?

(2) Read the picture story:

The bookshelf in my house is tall and holds many books, some pictures, and candles. It has big and small books.

There are also books for kids and books for parents. There is a picture of my mother and father, too.

There are two blue candles and a yellow candle. I am glad the books I like are on the lowest shelf.

A. Write the answers to the questions.

1. What type is the bookshelf?
2. What is on the bookshelf?
3. Whose photograph is on the bookshelf?
4. What is the color of the candles?

(3) Read the picture story:

The Parade

My mother took me and my brother Arun to the fun parade on Monday.

I saw three pretty white horses walking and some big dogs running in the parade.

The clowns and their puppies had on purple hats and big orange pants.

After the parade, the clowns gave me candy to eat. I ate my candy, and I clapped and clapped. It was a fun parade to see with my brother and mother.

A. Answer the following questions.

1. When did the mother and Arun go for a parade?

Answer: _______________________________________

2. Who gave candies to the children?

Answer: _______________________________________

3. What was the clown's puppy wearing?

Answer: _______________________________________

4. What did they all see in the fun parade?

Answer: ____

5. Write the describing words used in the passage for the following words.

________________Horses, ________________Dogs,

________________Hats, ________________Pants.

Reading Comprehension: Poems

(4) Read the poem carefully and answer the following questions.
Snow School Today

We bundle ourselves for it's time to leave.
The wind whips as we wait for Mr. Steve.
He rounds the corner in the yellow bus.
Opening the door, he calls out for us,
"It's cold this morning! Get in! The heat's on!"
We wave our goodbyes, and then we are gone.
The trip this morning is a slippery ride.
Look out the window; snow falls outside.
The street lights are blurry and glowing like jewels.
Beneath all our boots, snow melts into pools.
Now safe at school, we hear Mr. Steve say,

"Hurry inside now and keep warm today!"

1. Who is Mr. Steve?
Answer: ____

2. Which words best describe the weather in the poem?
      a) cold and rainy (   )
      b) snowing and calm ( )
      c) windy and cold (   )
      d) snowing and hailing (   )

3. The seventh line of the poem says: 'The trip this morning is a slippery ride.' What does this mean?
a) Kids are slipping when they get on the bus. (   )
b) The bus wheels are slipping on the ice. (   )
c) Kids are slipping and falling when they walk to the bus.( )
d) The bus floor is slippery. (   )

4. Write three words to describe Mr. Steve.
= ________________, ________________ and ________________.

5. How do the students probably feel on the bus?
      a) colder (   )
      b) warmer (   )
      c) tired (   )
      d) lost (   )

Moral Comprehension Passages

Some passages end with teaching some true lessons of life. Such passages are called Moral passages.

(5) Read the passage and answer the questions that follow.

There was a king in Scotland. His name was Robert Bruce. He fought many battles and won them. But once, he was badly defeated. He ran away from the battlefield to save his life. He took shelter in a cave where he hid himself. He lost all hope for

life.

But one day, he saw a spider trying to reach the cave roof, where it had a cobweb. It made six attempts to make its web, but every time, it slipped down. He was surprised to see that the spider did not lose heart but continued its efforts to reach the top. At the seventh attempt, the spider was successful in achieving its web.

This incident boosted King Bruce's spirit. He gained new strength and fresh courage. He fought another battle and ultimately freed his country from its enemies.

Moral: Keep trying until you succeed. The one who never stops making an effort is the one who ultimately wins.

Answer the following questions.

A. Arrange the jumbled words to make words.

1. bltate = <u>Battle</u>

2. mptsatte _________________

3. hlerste _________________

4. erdips _________________

5. bewcob _________________

B. Fill up the blanks.

1. King Bruce was the king of _________________

2. King took shelter in a _________________

3. He saw _________________ in the cave.

4. The spider was successful at the _________________ attempt.

5. The moral of the story is _________________________________.

C. State True/False.

1. The king's name was Robert Bruce. (   )

2. The king saw the lion in the cave. (   )

3. The spider made three attempts to reach its web. (   )

4. The spider incident boosted the spirit of the king. (   )

5. The story's moral is 'Do Not Try Again.' (   )

D. Look at the picture and name it.

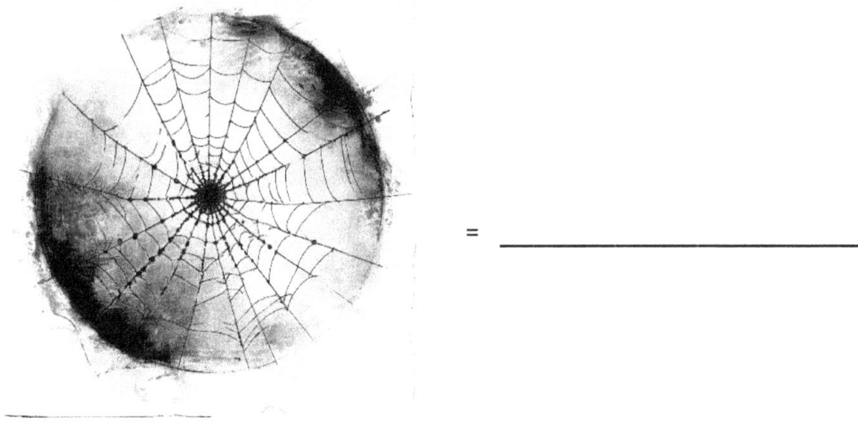

= _______________________________

Nonfiction Passages
Passage-1

(6) Read the passage and answer the following questions.

Going to the Movies

My class is going to the movies next week. We have to get permission slips signed before we go. We also need to ask our parents if they will drive us to the movie theatre. We are going to see a movie that tells the story of a book we read. We love it when movies are made from books. It is fun to compare movies to books. I usually like the book better. We get to the movie OUT early so we can buy popcorn. Some of us buy candy and slushes, too.

We all enjoy watching the movie. When we return to school, we talk about things that were in the movie and the book. The movie and book are similar, but we all agree that we like the book better. Books let you picture the characters any way you want.

Answer the following questions.
1. What do the students need to do before going to the movie?
2. What is fun to compare?
3. What do the students like better, the movie or the book?
4. What do the books let you do?

Nonfiction Passages: Passage-2

(7) Read the passage and answer the following questions.

'T' Time with Elephants

Three interesting things about elephants begin with the letter T — trunk, tusk, and teeth. An elephant's trunk has over forty thousand muscles and tendons. The trunk is a combination of the nose and the upper lip. An elephant uses its trunk to pick up things. It also uses its trunk for smelling. An elephant has two tusks. The tusks are made of ivory. The tusks grow from the elephant's upper jaw. An elephant has these two "teeth" instead of incisor teeth. The tusks grow throughout an elephant's life. An elephant uses its tusks to drill for water and to dig up food. All African elephants have tusks. Only some Asian male elephants have tusks. Some female Asian elephants also have tusks, which are very small and hidden inside their mouth.

An elephant also has four other teeth. These teeth are molars. An elephant has one upper molar and one lower molar on each side of its mouth. Because an elephant eats a lot of plants, its molars get ground down. New molars move in to replace the old molars about every ten years. An elephant gets up to six sets of molars over its lifetime.

Answer the following questions.

1. How many muscles and tendons are in an elephant's trunk?
       a. over 4,000 ( )
       b. over 40,000 ( )
       c. over 400,000 ( )
       d. over 40,000,000 ( )

2. What two things does an elephant use its trunk for?
= ______________________________________

3. What are two things an elephant uses its tusks for?

= ____________________________________

4. What does an elephant use its molars for?

        a. growing tusks ( )

        b. chewing plants ( )

        c. chewing small animals ( )

        d. speaking to another elephant ( )

Compare and Contrast Passages

(8) Read the passage.

Two Fantastic Fruits

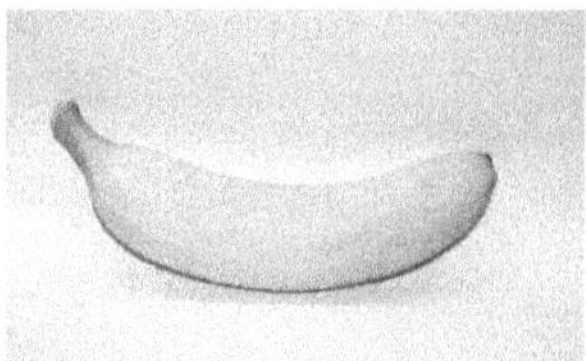

Bananas

Bananas are yellow fruits that grow in hot climates. They grow on tall plants in bunches called hands. They're easy to carry and fun to eat. Bananas are called the "perfect fruit" because they have many nutrients to keep you healthy. They have lots of potassium, which helps your muscles grow. For a delicious treat, add some banana slices to other foods, like cereal, ice cream, or a peanut butter sandwich. A banana is also an excellent breakfast food.

Pineapples

Pineapples are also yellow fruits that grow in hot climates. They grow on low plants close to the ground. Pineapples are very juicy and sweet. They are not easy to carry because they are big and have prickly skin. Pineapples are very healthy food. They have lots of vitamin C, which helps your body fight germs and helps build strong bones. Slices of pineapple taste wonderful when added to other foods, like pizza, ice cream, and hamburgers. Some people even put pineapple slices on cakes.

A. Tick the right option.

1. According to the paragraphs above, how are bananas and pineapples alike?

        a. They are both dirty fruits. ( )

        b. They both grow in bunches. ( )

        c. They are both easy to carry. ( )

        d. They both grow in hot climates. ( )

2. How are bananas and pineapples different?

    a. Pineapples are healthy, but bananas are not. ( )

    b. Bananas are easy to carry, but pineapples are not. ( )

    c. Pineapples grow on plants, but bananas do not. ( )

    d. Bananas and pineapples grow in hot climates. ( )

3. Which statement is an opinion?

    a. Some people put pineapple slices on cakes. ( )

    b. Bananas are a yellow fruit that grows in hot climates. ( )

c. Pineapples have prickly skin. ( )

d. Bananas taste delicious when added to cereal. ( )

B. What is a hand of bananas?

Ans: ____

ENGLISH GRAMMAR THROUGH THE READING SKILLS

Read through the Unseen Passages in Pictures. Answer the following questions based on your comprehension and use some grammar.

Arrangement of Words in Alphabetical Order

(1)   **Exercises.** Read the picture story.

Today is Maria's birthday. Maria's mother prepared a list of things required for her birthday party.

"Happy Birthday! Maria. Let's make a list of things for your birthday party.

We need **cake, candles, ice cream, caps**..." says Mumma. "**And balloons** and **gifts,** too," adds Maria.

"Let me pen down the list of all the things," says Mumma.

A. Will you now help Maria and her Mumma make a list of things in alphabetical order?

Ans: Alphabetically, the names of the articles will be thus,

____.

B. Answer the following questions.

1) Write the three things that start with the letter **C** alphabetically from the story above.

____

2) Name at least five friends you would like to invite to your birthday party. Write the names in alphabetical order.

____

3) From the list of Maria's mother, name the thing that would be at number three when arranged alphabetically by Maria's mother. _________________________

C. Directions: Read each pair of words. Write the word which would come first in alphabetical order.

Example: lost & found

Answer: found & lost

1. Run, walk − _______________________________
2. Play, sit − _______________________________
3. Fast, slow − _______________________________
4. Happy, smile − _______________________________
5. Face, arm − _______________________________
6. Look, swim − _________________
7. Jump, jog − _________________
8. Type, water − _________________
9. Friend, family − _________________
10. Stand, still − _________________

D. Read the words in each row. Then, arrange them in alphabetical order:

1） Need, plane, cute, cactus, truck, chase.

= ____

2） Plant, jeep, turtle, ship, cats, earth

= ____

3） Car, grow, little, train, mice, respect

= ____

Vowels and Consonants

(2)　　A balloon seller came into the colony, and he gave each child a balloon of a different color. Read the picture story:

A balloon seller comes to the colony.

He gives a red balloon to Arun and a yellow balloon to Mita.

"Where is mine?" asks Raju.

A. Answer the following questions from the story given above.

1. Who comes to the colony? __________________________
2. Which balloon does the balloon seller give to Mita?

----

3. Who gets the blue balloon? ___________________________

B. Underline the words that begin with vowels and circle the words that begin with consonants:

balloon, ear, yellow, red, elephant, blue, orange, inkjet, airplane,
seller

C. Add vowels to the following letters to correctly spell an animal's name. Write the name of the animal in the blanks. The first one has been done for you.

1. Ms = <u>Mouse</u>
2. Brd = ___________
3. Lmb = ___________
4. Hrs = ___________
5. Snk = ___________
6. Tgr = ___________
7. Rbbt = ___________

D. Color the candy red if it has a vowel. Yellow if it has a consonant in it.

E. Fill in the blanks with the missing vowels and consonants.

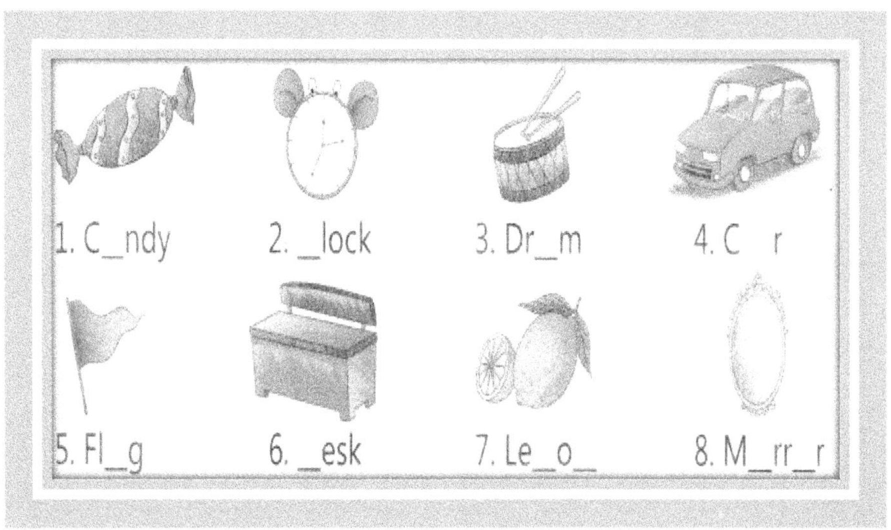

Naming Words and Pronouns: 'He' Names & 'She' Names

(3)   In the following, study Nouns and Pronouns through the picture story:

I am Vikram. Call **me** Vicky.

We are students. Tell **us** a story.

She is my sister. I love **her** very much.

He is my brother. I love **him** very much.

You are my student. I tell **you** stories.

They are our parents. We love **them** dearly.

It is a pencil. Sharpen **it**, please.

They are our cows. We give **them** good grass.

You are my friend. Let me give **you** a pen.

It is a cat. Give **it** some milk.

(4)   Read the following story and answer the questions:

"Hi Anjan, can you come to my house to play with me? We can play chess, ludo, and other games," asks Sanjukta.

"My Mother wants me to do my homework. She will let me play only after I finish it," replies Anjan.

"Fine... I will play with my dog till you come. It can run and catch my ball. You can join us after you finish your homework."

says Sanjukta.

A. Answer the following questions.

1. What does Sanjukta ask Anjan?

____

2. Why does Anjan's mother not allow her to play?

____

3. Which naming word is used in place of dog?

____

B. From the story above, write naming words for the following pronouns or other names.

a. We _______________________

b. She _______________________

c. It _______________________

d. Us ___________________

C. Fill in the blanks with a suitable pronoun (the words used in place of Nouns). You may choose from the list given in the box:

(*Him, Her, It, They, He, She, them*) :

1. **Mr. Rohit** is a policeman. _______________ catches thieves.
2. **Ms. Reena** is a teacher. _____________ teaches in a school.
3. **Boys and girls** go to school. _______ learn to read and write.
4. **The elephant** is a wild animal. ___________ lives in a jungle.
5. I have **a piece of meat.** I will give _____________ to the dog.
6. **My father** loves me, and I love _______________ too.
7. I have **many books.** I keep _______________ in my bag.
8. **My mother** is charming. I love _______________ a lot.

D. Here are two sets of pronoun forms. One set is used before doing words and another after doing words or verbs. Draw a line to join each one with the other, used in place of.

I	he	it	she	they	you	we
Us	her	you	them	me	him	it

E. Fill in the blanks with correct pronouns instead of the bold words. Pronouns you may choose from the above.

1. **Pawan and I** are brothers. _________ share a bedroom.
2. **Suman** isn't well. Dad is taking ______ to see a doctor.
3. **My brother** is a teacher. _________ teaches English.
4. All **his** students like _________ very much.
5. **Children** _________ are making noise will be punished?

(*use either* **'who,' 'whose,'** *or* **'whom'**)

6. Who are those **people**? Where are _________ from?
7. **Mom** is a doctor. _________ works in a hospital.

8. The sky is getting dark. ___________ is going to rain.

F. Tick the correct pronoun option against the bold words on the left.

		Tick at the right box.			*Tick at the right box.*
	He			He	
Peter is planning his project.	She		**Gita** is reading a book.	She	
		Tick at the right box			*Tick at the right box*
	He			He	
The **old man** is walking with a stick.	She		My **mother** is a renowned singer.	She	

G. Write now 5 'He' names looking around you that denote male names.

    1. ___________________________

    2. ___________________________

    3. ___________________________

    4. ___________________________

    5. ___________________________

H. Write here 5 'She' names looking around you that denote female names.

    1. ___________________________

2. _______________________

3. _______________________

4. _______________________

5. _______________________

Doing or Action Words

(5) **Look at the picture given below. Write a sentence using _a pronoun_ to answer each question about the image.**

Questions:

1. What is the boy doing? =

____

2. What is the girl doing? =

____

3. Where is the monkey? =

____

4. What is the color of the sky? =

____

5. What are the old man and the old woman doing? =

____

6. What are the birds doing? =

____

Names and Describing Words

(6)   Circle the describing word and underline the names.

Full moon   Evil witch   Big pumpkin

Sweet candy   Green Monster   Spooky house

Black bat   Pale vampire   Fun costume

Look at the pictures and tick the correct sentences.

	The train is fast. ( )	The train is slow. ( )
	The moon is half. ( )	The moon is full. ( )
	Winters are hot. ( )	Winters are cold. ( )
	The car is red. ( )	The car is white. ( )
	The wood is hard. ( )	The wood is soft. ( )
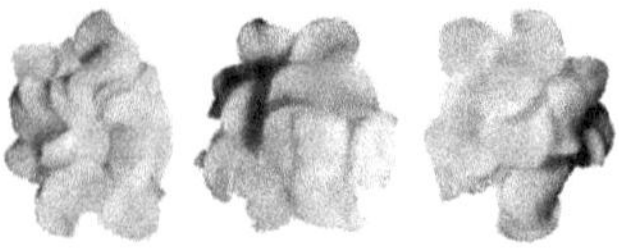	Chips taste salty. ( )	The chips taste sweet. ( )

Comparisons in Describing Words: Use of Degrees

Study the examples.

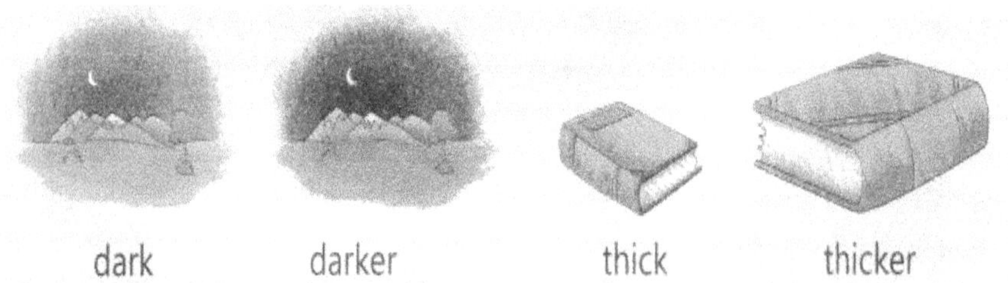

Read, when we use **'More' before a describing word**, generally after a longer word.

Examples:-

beautiful   **more** beautiful

active	**more** active
charming	**more** charming
cheerful	**more** cheerful
comfortable	**more** comfortable
delicious	**more** delicious

(7)   Read the picture story.

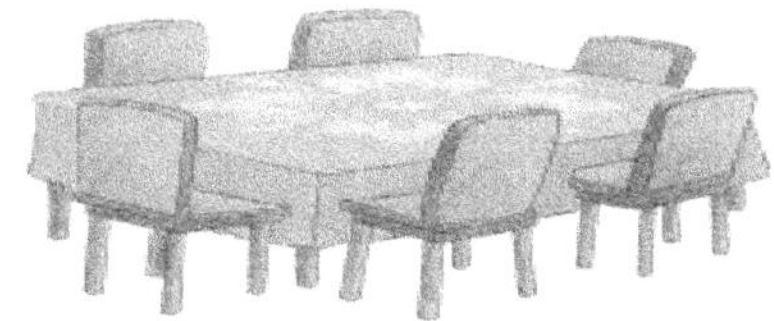

"Do you like this big dining table?" Harshabardhan asks. "Wow! That's great. This is bigger than the one at our home," says Rita.

"Do you like the tablecloth?" asks Harsha. "Well... I must say it is more beautiful and prettier than the table," says Rita.

"Shall we buy it? It's not so expensive. It is cheaper than the other tables we saw," asks Rita. "Okay, let's ask the shopkeeper," says Harsha.

A. Answer the following questions.

1. Which word does Harsha use to describe the table?
2. Which words does Rita use to describe the tablecloth?
3. Is the table expensive?

B. Write the positive forms of words given below.

1. _____________ = bigger

2. _____________ = more beautiful

3. _____________ = prettier

4. _____________ = more expensive

5. _____________ = cheaper

6. _____________ = costlier

C. Circle the correct describing word for each picture.

D. Write the *correct form of the describing word* and its preposition, *'than,'* where necessary. You may also use *'more'* where required.

1. Ram is ______________ Rita. (tall)

2. A pen is ______________ a sword. (useful)
3. Sarita is ______________ her sister. (young)
4. This dress is ______________ that dress. (beautiful)
5. Mangoes are ______________ apples. (cheap)

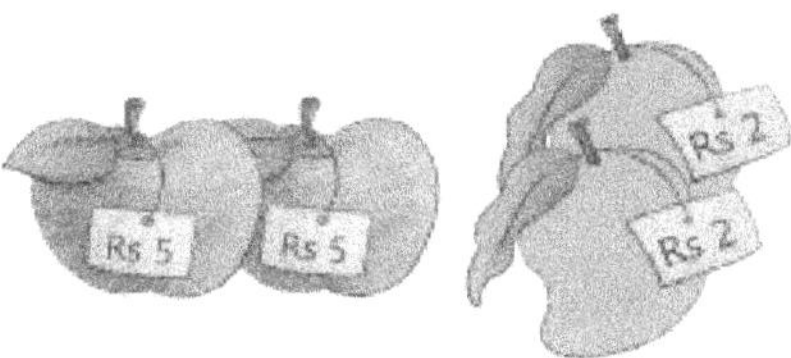

6. Iron is ______________ wood. (heavy)
7. Mr. Thakur was ______________ Mr. Paul. (wealthy)

8. A car runs _____________ a bicycle. （fast）

Describing Numbers

(8)   Read the picture story.

Nine girls from our class are selected for the Annual Day function.

Three girls are selected for the dance performance, two girls are chosen for the solo performance, and four girls are selected to participate in the debate competition.

Only a few participants will receive distinguished prizes. However, participation certificates will be given to all the selected girls.

A. Answer the following questions as per the story.

1. How many girls are selected for solo performance?

____

2. How many girls are selected for dance performance?

____

3. Which describing words of number are used to represent the selected girls of the class?

____

B. Quick Prompts

1. How many months are there in a year? _______________
2. How many days are there in a week? _______________
3. How many players are there in a cricket team?

____

4. How many colors does a traffic light have? _______________
5. How many colors are there in a rainbow? _______________

C. Underline the describing number words in the following sentences.

1. I have three books.
2. He ate a few bananas.
3. Kishore drank two glasses of milk.
4. A house has four walls.
5. All the students were present.

The Use of Possessive Adjectives

(9)   **Read the picture story.**

We are going to celebrate a party. "My idea is to serve egg sandwiches," says Rohit. "I like his idea because eggs are pretty easy to cook," says Varun.

"My idea is to serve cheeseburgers," says Nancy. "Does anyone else have a better idea?" asks Rohit. "Bunny, tell us your idea if you have any?" says Nancy.

"Everyone wants their favorite dish. However, I like chicken curry," says Bunny.

"Hey, don't forget Manu and Richa. They also have an idea for the party to serve pizzas," says Varun.

"I like pizza. It's my favorite food. I like their idea", says Nancy.

"I think I like Bunny's idea," says Rohit.

A. Answer the following questions as per the story.

1. What food does Rohit suggest for the party?
2. Who likes Manu and Richa's suggestion?
3. What do you think, whose suggestion is the best?

B. Write the name of the food the boys prefer for their party.

1. Manu and Richa ______________
2. Bunny ______________
3. Rohit ______________
4. Varun ______________
5. Nancy ______________

C. Fill in the blanks with 'my,' 'your,' 'his,' 'her,' 'him,' 'its,' 'our,' or **'their.'**

1. Would you lend me ___________ book?

2. Return Madhu ___________ book.

3. You and Madhu, submit ___________ projects with the class teacher by tomorrow.

4. Nandita has lost ___________ purse.

5. The machine is useless without ___________ cord.

6. Hari, Raju, and Reena; ask them to be here with ___________ parents.

8. We love ___________ team.

9. The boy has given ___________ test.

10. My daughter has put on ___________ shoes

11. Ask ___________ to be here in time.

12. Return me ___________ test book.

The Use of Articles: 'A,' 'An,' & 'The'

PRESENTATION

(10)   Read the picture story.

A. Answer the following questions as per the story.

   1. Name the fruits that the boy had.

2. Which fruit did Rahul eat?

3. Which fruit did the boy eat?

B. Complete the sentences by writing *'a'*, *'an'*, or *'the'* in the blanks.

1. ________________ tortoise and ________________ hare were neighbors. One day, ________________ hare challenged ________________ tortoise to ________________ race. However, finally, tortoise won ________________ race.

2. I have ________________ dog and ________________ parrot as pets. ________ dog is always quiet, but ________________ parrot is noisy.

C. Write a few sentences about each picture. Remember, *'a'* and *'an'* are to be used when writing about one naming word, and use 'the' when you repeat the name.

Example

A

B

C

D. Write *'a'* and *'an'* before each of these words. Pay attention to the sound and not just the first letter.

1. ________________ European

2. ________________ house

3. ________________ useless dress

4. ________________ umbrella

5. _______________ unicorn

6. _______________ hour and a half

7. _______________ unhappy man

8. _______________ honest boy

Identifying Pictures with Proper 'Doing Words'

A. Look at the pictures and put a (X) mark against wrong answers.

(1) Eating food (   );

Cooking food (   )

(2) Playing cricket (   );

Playing football (   )

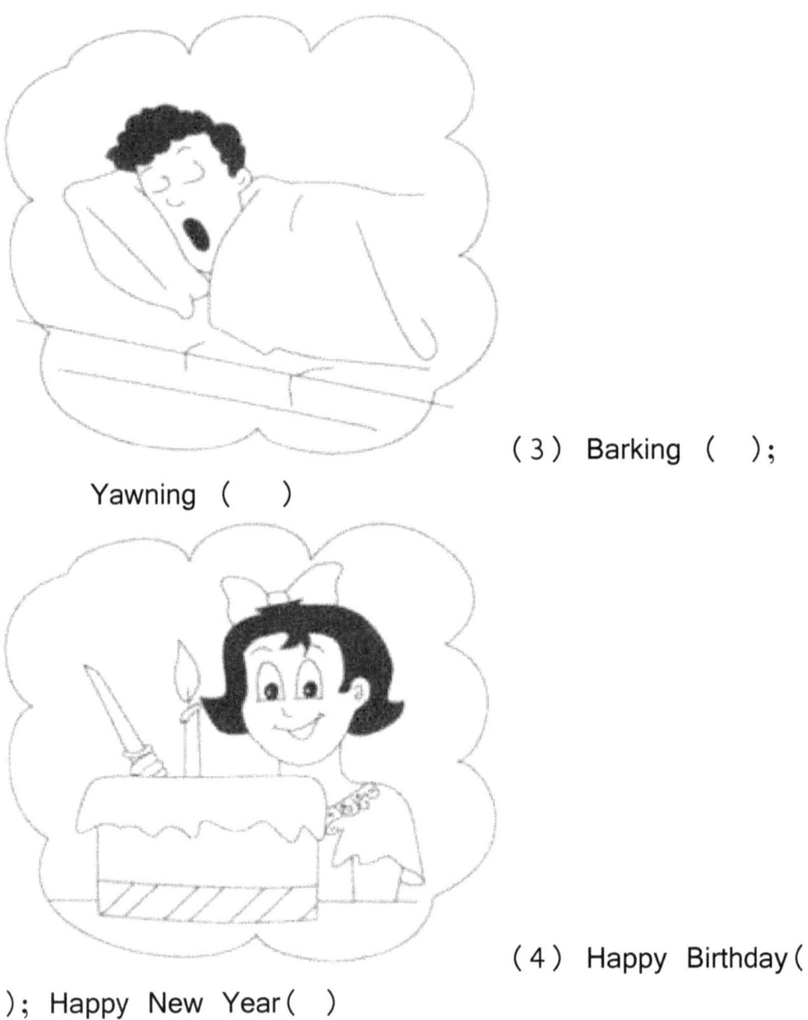

（3） Barking （ ）;

Yawning （   ）

（4） Happy Birthday（

）; Happy New Year（ ）

B. Look at the pictures and fill in the blanks with verbs given within brackets.

(punch, taste, walk, catch, see, hear, eat, smell)

You _______________ with your tongue. You _______________ with your fist.

You _______________ with your hands. You _______________ with your nose.

You _______________ with your ears. You _______________ with your legs.

You _______________ with your eyes. You _______________ with your mouth.

The '-ing' Form of Verbs

PRESENTATION

(11)   Read the picture story.

Nancy is visiting her grandparents. At this moment, she is sitting on her grandfather's knee, listening to a story. She loves her grandfather's story very much.

Mr. Gopal is Nancy's grandfather. He ¡s holding her hands. They are sitting in the living room. Right now, he ¡s telling her a story. They enjoy each other's company.

Mrs. Gopal is Nancy's grandmother. She is standing in the kitchen and baking cookies for Nancy and her grandfather. She ¡s also listening to the story.

A. Answer the following questions.

   1. Who is Nancy visiting today? ________________

2. Where are Mr. Gopal and his granddaughter sitting?
____

3. What is Mrs. Gopal doing? _______________

B. Fill in the blanks with the *-ing form of the verb* from the story above.

- Visit _____________   Hold _____________   Listen _____________
- Live _____________   Tell _____________   Stand _____________
- Sit _____________   Bake _____________

C. Add 'ing' to the following doing words. *(Remove the letter 'e' from the verb before adding '-ing' if the verb ends with '-e')*

- Come _____________   Run _____________   Ask _____________
- Sleep _____________   Catch _____________   Fall _____________
- Meet _____________   Jump _____________   Drop _____________
- Bring _____________   Climb _____________   Live _____________
- Go _____________   Slide _____________   Move _____________
- Cook _____________   Sit _____________   Stand _____________
- Write _____________   Read _____________   Play _____________

D. Fill in the blanks with the correct doing word and helping verb. (present continuous = am/is/are + -ing doing word)

1. They _____________ the roller-coaster ride. (enjoy)
2. Jiya _____________ her hair. (wash)
3. It _____________ dark. (get)
4. The dentist _____________ Suman's teeth. (examine)
5. The train _____________ through the tunnel. (pass)

E. Match the pictures with the correct actions and tick the right box.

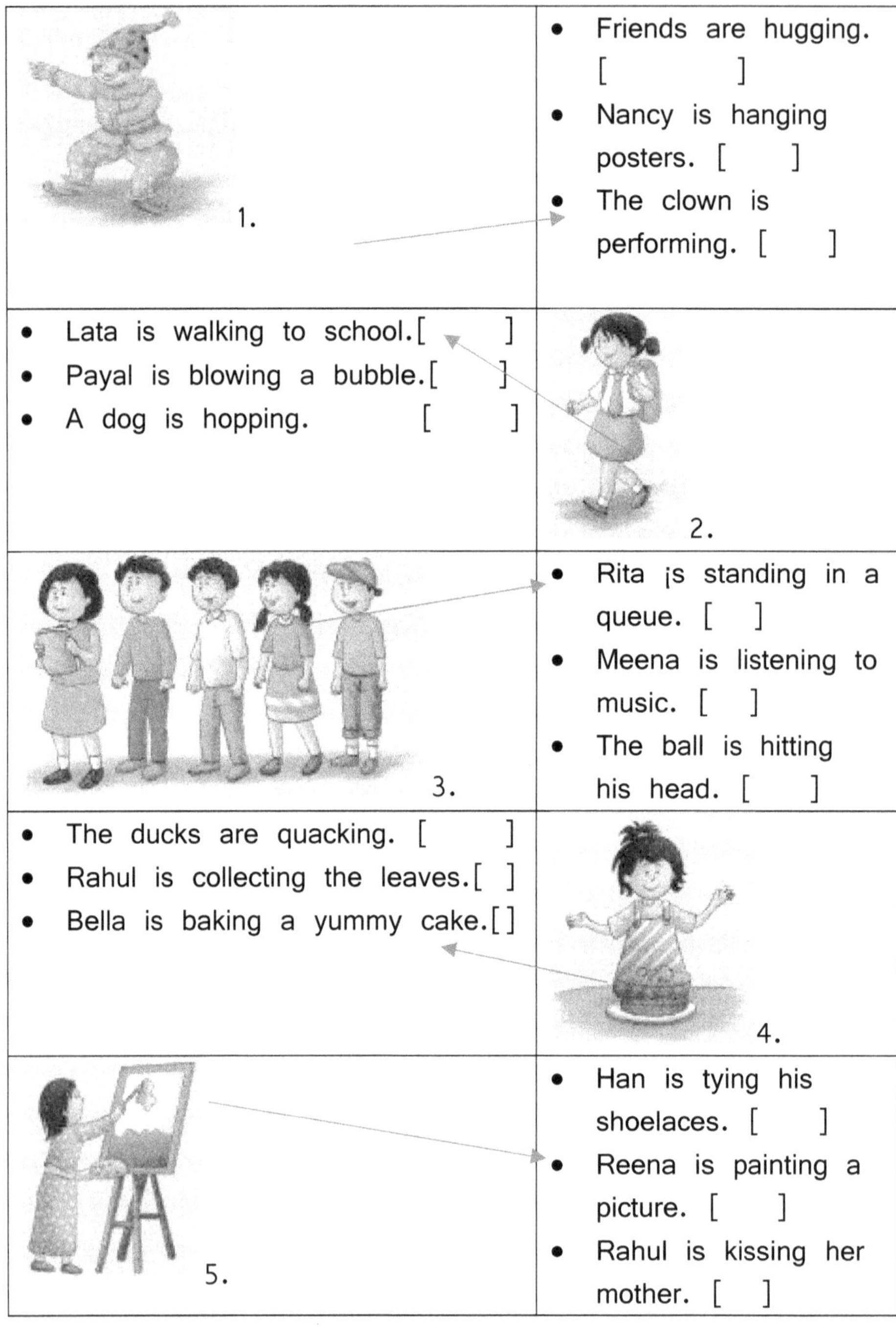

1.
• Friends are hugging. [   ]
• Nancy is hanging posters. [   ]
• The clown is performing. [   ]
• Lata is walking to school. [   ]
• Payal is blowing a bubble. [   ]
• A dog is hopping. [   ]
2.
• Rita is standing in a queue. [   ]
• Meena is listening to music. [   ]
• The ball is hitting his head. [   ]
3.
• The ducks are quacking. [   ]
• Rahul is collecting the leaves. [   ]
• Bella is baking a yummy cake. [ ]
4.
• Han is tying his shoelaces. [   ]
• Reena is painting a picture. [   ]
• Rahul is kissing her mother. [   ]
5.

- Raju is shutting the door. [   ]
- Sohan is rushing to work. [   ]
- Mita is working hard.   [   ]

6.

The '–d' and '–ed' Forms of Verbs & Other Past Forms

PRESENTATION

(12)   Read the picture story.

Last week, Bunny baked a cake for Lilly's birthday party. Lilly wanted a strawberry cake with pink frosting.

First, Bunny mixed the ingredients in a big bowl and baked the cake for 20 minutes. He prepared the pink frosting. Lastly, he wrote Lilly's name on top with white frosting. Last, he put seven candles on the cake.

On Sunday, Bunny surprised Lilly with the strawberry cake. Lilly loved her cake! Lilly received many gifts on her birthday, but she said the cake was the best gift of them all!

A. Answer the following questions from the story above.

1. What did Bunny do for Lilly's birthday party?
2. What did Bunny prepare?
3. What did Lilly like best among her birthday gifts?

B. Add −ed to the following doing words. Remember, *when the word ends with '−e,'* add only '−d' to the doing word.

Bake ________________

Prepare ________________

Love ________________

Want ________________

Mix ________________

Surprise ________________

C. Complete each sentence by adding −ed to the doing words given in the brackets.

1. My dad (craft) ________________ a boat.
2. He (mow) ________________ the grass.
3. I (watch) ________________ television in the morning.
4. Sameer (pick) ________________ up the journal today.
5. We (serve) ________________ lunch at 12.30.
6. Grandma (bake) ________________ the best cookies.
7. He (paint) ________________ the house.
8. Sarika (cook) ________________ the breakfast.
9. Pawan (play) ________________ the piano at the concert.
10. I ________________ (open) my book yesterday.

The Use of 'Am,' 'Is,' 'Are,' & 'Was,' and 'Were'

Presentation

(13)   Read the picture story.

A. Answer the following questions from the story given above.

1. What did the children do in the snowfall? _______________

2. What did the people wear in Manali? _______________

3. Was the hotel room cold or warm? _______________

B. Fill in the blanks with 'was' or 'were.'

It _________ holiday yesterday. The school _______________ closed and the shops _________ closed. We _______________ at home. It _______________ fun.

C. Fill in the blanks with 'was' or 'were.'

1. We _______________ the champions last year.

2. I _______________ in class I last year.

3. Mom and Dad _______________ were on vacation last week.

4. The weather _______________ fine this morning.

5. There ________________ a lot of people at our party yesterday.
6. There ________________ a small lake here many years ago.
7. He ________________ sick yesterday.
8. Don't blame him. It ________________ my mistake.

D. Write *was* or *were* in the blank spaces in the following passage.

It ________________ a beautiful day, and there ________________ not a cloud in the sky. Mom, Dad, and I ________________ in the garden. Dad ________________ in the vegetable garden planting some seeds, and Mom and I ________________ busy with other jobs. The sun ________________ hot and soon I ________________ feeling very tired. Mom and Dad ________________ not tired at all. They went on working for a long time. I ________________ glad when it ________________ time to go inside and have a drink together.

(14)   Fill in the blanks with *is, am, are, was, were*.

1. Tom ________________ in the garden yesterday.

2. The eggs ________________ in the box now.

3. Sugar ________________ the packet.

4. There ________________ hot coffee in the cup.

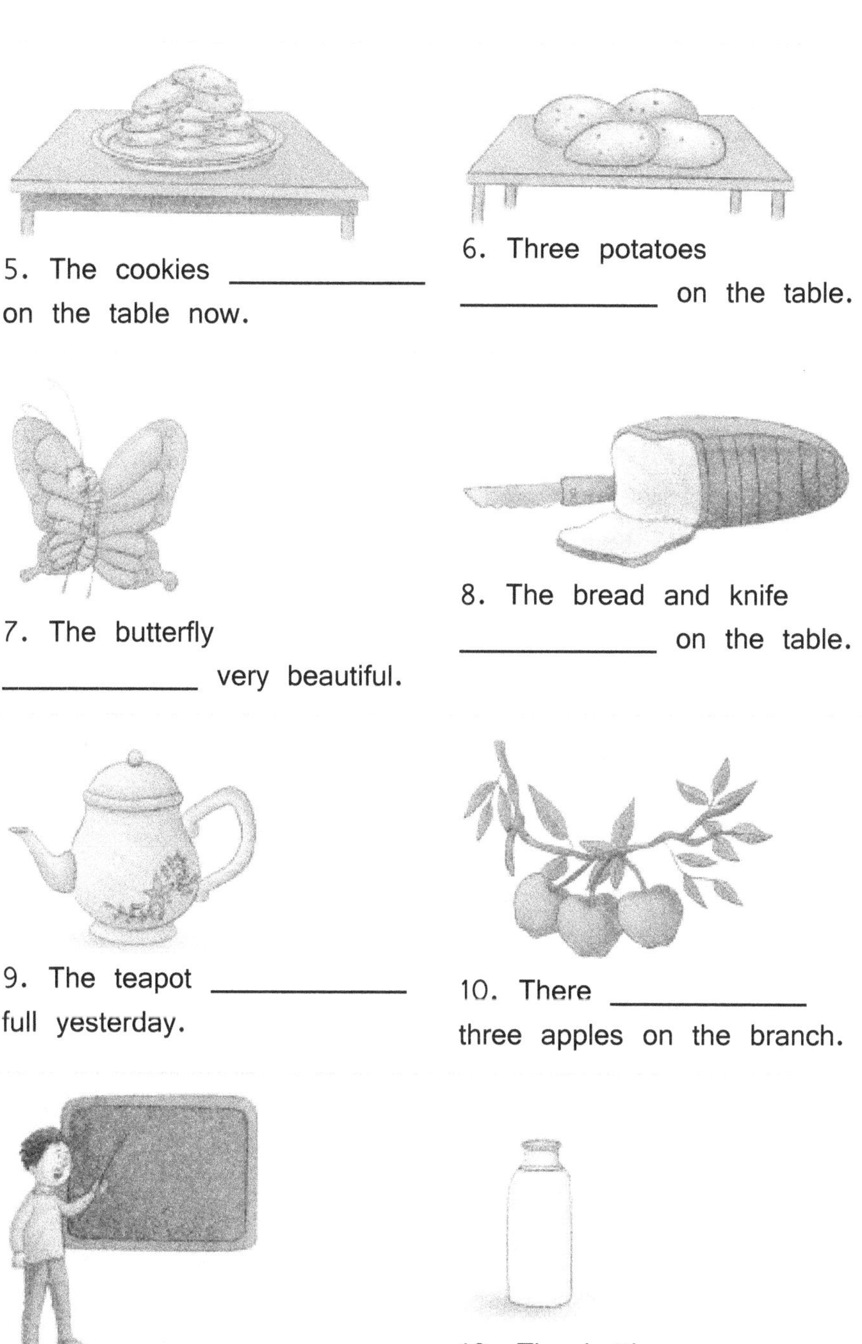

5. The cookies ______________ on the table now.

6. Three potatoes ______________ on the table.

7. The butterfly ______________ very beautiful.

8. The bread and knife ______________ on the table.

9. The teapot ______________ full yesterday.

10. There ______________ three apples on the branch.

11. I ______________ writing the blackboard yesterday.

12. The bottle ______________ full of milk yesterday.

13. There ______________ two apples in the kitchen.

14. Bill ______________ crying now.

15. Paul ______________ rowing the boat two hours ago.

16. Pam ______________ sitting on the floor now.

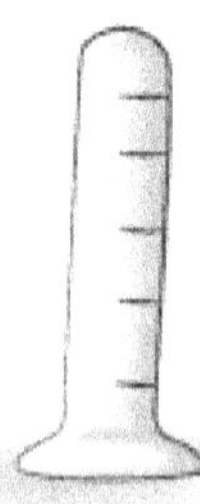

17. It ______________ very hot yesterday.

18. It ______________ raining today.

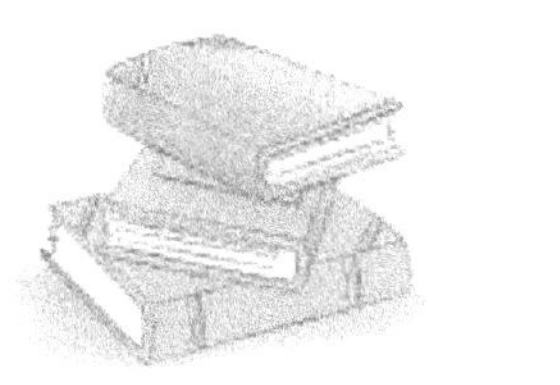

19. The books ____________ new.

20. Mona ____________ cooking now.

PRESENTATION 2

(15)   Read the picture story.

This is a picture of our sea beach trip. We went for a picnic at the beach. The crab was crawling near the sea, and the dolphin behind the boat was jumping out of the water.

On the beach, chairs were beside the table. The little girl was sitting in front of the sand castle, and the beach ball was lying between the girls.

Across the sea, the boy was in the parachute. The sun was shining above the sea.

A. Answer the following questions as per the story.

1. Where was the crab in the story?

____

2. Where was the beach ball?

____

3. What was behind the boat in the picture?

____

B. Look at the picture story again and state whether the following statements are true or false.

1. The dolphin is under the water. _______________
2. The crab is near the sea. _______________
3. The boat is below the tree. _______________
4. The little girl is in between the sandcastle. _______________

The Use of 'Had' and '−ed' Forms of Verbs

PRESENTATION

(16)   Read the picture story.

Last night, Mona and Sonu danced in a competition. They had practiced for six months before the competition and were very good.

Mona and Sonu's friends were in the audience. Before that night, they had never seen Mona and Sonu's dance.

After everyone had danced, the judges announced the winners.
Mona and Sonu won! They were the best dancers in the
competition. Mona was glad they had practiced a lot.

A. **Answer the following questions.**

1. What did Mona and Sonu do in the competition?

____

2. Who was present in the audience?

____

3. What did the judges announce at the end of the competition?

____

B. **Use the** *'had'* **and** *'– ed'* **forms of verbs** and other forms of
verbs, like past and progressive tense in the past, where
necessary, to complete the following sentences. (*The use of*

past perfect tense is when an action was completed in the past.）

1. When their mother _______________ （come） home last night, the children _______________ （eat） their dinner.

2. Yesterday I _______________ （see） a woman who _______________ （be） at school with my grandfather. Wasn't it strange?

3. It started to rain, and I _______________ （remember） that I _______________ （forget） to close my bedroom window.

4. I _______________ （find） a book that I never _______________ （read）.

C. **Fill in the blanks using the verbs** *'Had'* and *'-ed'* **forms at the end of the doing verbs.**
   1. When I arrived at the cinema, the film _______________ （start）.
   2. She _______________ （live） in China before she went to Thailand.
   3. After they _______________ （eat） the shellfish, they began to feel sick.
   4. If you _______________ （listen） to me, you would have got the job.
   5. After we _______________ （finish） dinner, we went out.

The Use of 'How Words' or Adverbs

PRESENTATION

(17)   Read the picture story.

Mohit has enthusiastically participated in the Writing Olympiad. He practiced for this competition seriously.

He practiced silently. During the competition, he wrote slowly and neatly. He used his words artistically.

Humbly and Kindly, the Judges announced the result, with Mohit as the winner. "Well Done! Mohit." Mohit accepted his trophy happily.

A. Answer the following questions from the story above.

   1. How did Mohit practice? _______________

2. How did Mohit write? _______________

3. How did Mohit accept the trophy? _______________

B. Describe the way you do things.

1. How do you think? _______________

2. How do you fight? _______________

3. How do you sing? _______________

4. How do you dance? _______________

5. How do you walk? _______________

C. Look at the pictures. Choose the correct *'How' Word* from the box to fill in the blanks.

neatly, angrily, quickly, sadly, slowly, heavily, happily, brightly, loudly, beautifully

1. Laugh _______________

2. Run _______________

3. Shout _______________

4. Sun ______________

5. Walk ______________

6. Cry ______________

7. Smile ______________

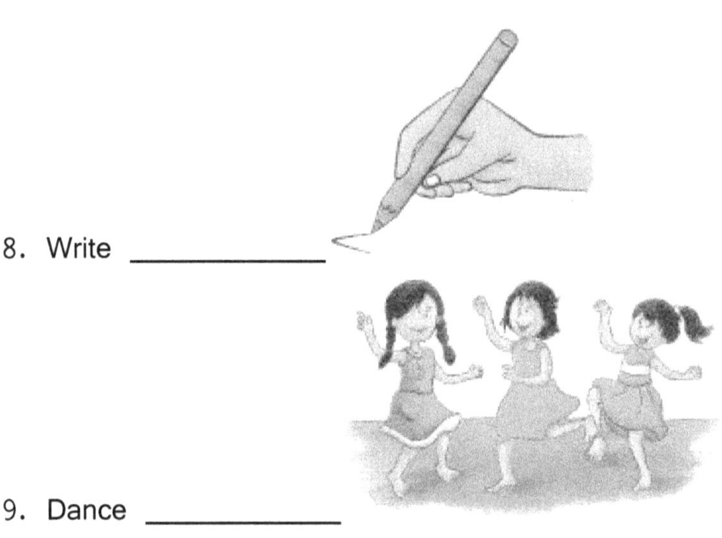

8. Write __________

9. Dance __________

D. Tick the correct word.

1. She could hard/hardly walk after the accident.
2. I live near/nearly the supermarket.
3. We will go on a vacation short/shortly.
4. She is too short/shortly. She cannot be a model.
5. The quiz was easy/easily.

[Submit the copy with your teacher.]

E. Make 'how words' by adding -ly: For example: Slow - Slowly.

1. Careful − __________
2. Quick − __________
3. Loud − __________
4. Terrible − __________
5. Weak − __________
6. Happy − __________

F. Choose the correct option to complete the sentences.

1. I like to live in a ___________

house.   clean (   ) / cleanly (   )

2. Rashi usually sings ___________.   happy (   )
/happily (   )

3. Madhuri is a ___________ girl.   beautiful (   )
/beautifully (   )

4. Reena speaks English ___________.
fluent (   ) / fluently (   )

5. Sahil ran ____________ fast ( ) / fastly (   )

G. Choose the correct prepositions to complete the sentences given below.

1. A newspaper is ____________ the pillow. (in, on, under)

2. A ball is ____________ the car. (in, on, under)

3. Clothes are ____________ the closet. (in, on, under)

4. A cat is ____________ the chair. (in, on, under)

5. Candy is _______________   6. Shells are _______________
the bag. (in, on, under)   the stool. (in, on, under)

The Words that show 'Relations,' i.e. Prepositions

**(18)   Study the picture and state whether the following statements
are 'true' or 'false.'**

1. The chair is next to the desk _______________________
2. The bed is opposite to the window. _______________
3. The computer is under the desk. _______________
4. The bookcase is on the wall. _______________
5. The bin is between the bed and the desk. _______________
6. The lamp is on the desk. _______________
7. The poster is above the shelf. _______________
8. The window is above the bed. _______________
9. The clock is on the bed. _______________

(19)   Look at the picture and, again, fill in the blanks.

1. The carpet is on the floor.
2. The elephant poster is _____________ the wall.
3. The clothes are _____________ the wardrobe.
4. The photo is _____________ the clock and the plant.
5. The doll house is _____________ the wardrobe.
6. The bookcase is _____________ the sofa.
7. The shelf is _____________ the wardrobe.
8. The pencil cup is _____________ desk.
9. The chair is _____________ the desk.
10. The elephant poster is _____________ the panda poster.
11. The bag is _____________ the desk.

Exercise: Fill in the following blanks with correct prepositions.

1. He climbed _____________ the hills.
2. My family usually eats dinner _____________ 8.00 pm.
3. Look _____________ the street before crossing.
4. There is a mango tree _____________ the lake.
5. My father took grapes _____________ of his bag.
6. The boy was standing _____________ the curtain.
7. The bench is _____________ the tree.
8. Neha and Vivek are playing _____________ of their house.
9. There is a fence _____________ the house.
10. We have beautiful flowers _____________ the garden.

The Use of 'And,' 'But,' & 'Or'

Read the examples given below.

The boy **and** the girl are wearing hats.

I like ice cream, **but** I'm not too fond of milk.

I will have milk **or** honey.

PRESENTATION

(20) Read the picture story.

Hummingbirds are tiny and colorful. Their legs are weak, but their wings are strong. Their wings beat fast and make a humming sound.

The birds can fly up or down, backward or sideways, hang in the air, or drink nectar from a flower.

They usually lay two eggs, and their babies are featherless. Grass, bark, or cobwebs hold their nest together. It's really amazing!

A. Answer the following questions as per the story.

1. Describe Hummingbirds?

Answer: ____

2. What have you learned about Humming bird's legs and wings from the story?

Answer: ____

3. From where does Hummingbird drink nectar?

Answer: ____

B. Fill in each blank with a word from the story above.

1. Hummingbirds make a humming sound with their ___________

2. Hummingbirds can fly up _____________ down, backward ______________ sideways.

3. ______________, bark or ____________ hold the nest together.

GRAMMAR EXERCISE:

A. Fill in the blanks with *'and'* **or** *'but'* :

1. Vijay is tall __________ thin. 2. Raju is tall, ______ not thin.

3. I found the book, __________ I can't find the pen.

4. I have found the book __________ pen.

5. The dog ____________ the cat are fighting.

6. The dog is sleeping ____________ the cat is not.

B. Use 'or' to join the following. The first one has been done for you.

1. Do you like tea? Do you like coffee?

Answer: I like tea, but not coffee.

1. Is your shirt red? Is your shirt green?

Answer: ___________________________

2. Is that Meera? Is that Rita?

Answer: ___________________________

3. Is a tiger stronger? Is a lion stronger?

Answer: ___________________________

4. Do you like a burger? Do you like a pizza?

Answer: ___________________________

C. Complete the sentences with correct conjunctions.

1. My grandma makes tasty cakes _______ snacks for us all. **(and, but)**

2. Her writing is good, ____________ her spellings are weak. **(and, but)**

3. Anuj ____________ Sunny are playing on the beach. **(and, but)**

4. Rita fell down, ____________ she did not get hurt. **(and, but)**

D. Circle the joining words in the following sentences.

1. They walked and played in the park.
2. I like popcorn, but my sister likes chips.
3. Mohit hoped to get a baseball or video game for his birthday.
4. Nina knocked at the door, but no one answered.
5. We saw clowns, horses, and elephants at the circus.
6. Who will go with us? Mita or Gita?

Antonyms or Opposite Words

- The **opposite words** are also known as '**antonyms.**'
- Words that *have completely different meanings* are called opposite words.

. Match the words in column A with their opposites in column B:

a) Bad	1) Good
b) Bitter	2) Shallow
c) Begin	3) Awake
d) Build	4) Common
e) Bent	5) Destroy
f) Lend	6) Short
g) Worst	7) Sweet

h) Rare	8) Straight
i) Deep	9) Cruel
j) Sleep	10) Best
k) Kind	11) Borrow
l) Tall	12) End

About Author

Mr. Peter is a teacher and professional author of numerous academic books on English Grammar and Writing Skills. Additionally, he has authored various works, including stories, novels, and poems. Some of his works also collaborate with Mr. Sarkar and others, authors from Bharat (formerly India). Mr. Peter's books have been published on global platforms like Amazon, Notion Press, and Google. These books are accessible in various formats like eBooks, audiobooks, paperbacks, and hardcovers on Amazon Kindle, Google Play Store, and Google Books, as well as on Flipkart and Amazon.

On the web browsers and platforms mentioned, one can easily search by the book title or author's name to locate his works. Thank you, and best of Luck.

Some important works by the writer & Co-author:

1. Study of Nouns, Pronouns, Adjectives & Articles (detail study) ISBN: 979-832-697-263-7 / 979-832-697-510-2
2. All about Verbs (Forms, Functions, Conjugation, Tense, Voice Change, Forming Questions & Negation) ISBN: 979-832-807-531-2 / 979-832-807-688-3
3. Study of Adverbs, Prepositions, Conjunctions & Interjections ISBN: 979-832-886-943-0 / 979-883-987-196-0
4. Detail Study of Phrases, Clauses & Sentences, including Idioms & Phrasal Verbs ISBN: 979-832-939-104-6 / 979-884-011-097-3
5. Study of Subject-Verb Agreement, Narration Change, and Use of Punctuation, including Analysis, Synthesis, & Split-up (Study through charts, division, explanation, and examples) ISBN: 979-880-723-013-3 / 979-888-704-674-7
6. **Peter's 'English Grammar, A Complete Version of English Grammar,** (detail study, explanation & examples) ISBN: 979-879-725-020-3 / 979-888-704-463-7
7. **Question Bank of English Grammar & Composition** (Learn through Exercises) ISBN: 979-883-531-890-2 / 979-888-733-132-4
8. **Rhetoric & Prosody** (A handbook of Figures of Speech, rhymes, feet of poetic lines for High School Students) ISBN: 979-840-526-645-9 / 979-888-684-952-3
9. **A Book of Advanced Writing Skill, the Complete Version** (incl Part-1, 2 & 3) ISBN: 979-836-472-826-5 / 979-888-869-835-8
10. **English** *Grammar* **& Question Bank Together** For Class VI to XII (Learn through Exercise) ISBN 979-838-571-382-0
11. **New English Pal,** Class **10** (A Complete Guide Book for Smart Learning, based on WBBSE syllabus) by **P. Sarkar, based on Peter's Grammar and Composition**: [Separate book for each class from 5 to 10]
12. **The Rainbow** (A Collection of Short Stories) ISBN 10: 979-832141310-4; 979-832141545-0 & ISBN 13: 979-889363024-4

Author page URL's:

https://www.amazon.com/author/mr.peter

https://www.amazon.in/~/e/B09QW2P4TY (Bharat/India)

https://www.amazon.co.uk/~/e/B09QW2P4TY

https://www.amazon.de/~/e/B09QW2P4TY

https://www.amazon.fr/~/e/B09QW2P4TY

https://www.amazon.co.jp/~/e/B09QW2P4TY

https://www.amazon.es/~/e/B09QW2P4TY

https://www.amazon.it/~/e/B09QW2P4TY

https://www.amazon.com.br/kindle-dbs/entity/author?asin=B09QW2P4TY

In Bharat/India, you can purchase the paperback version of my book by visiting notionpress.com and typing the author's name or title of a book in the search box. You may also use these links:

https://www.facebook.com/groups/mr.peter,

https://notionpress.com/store/s?NP_Books%5Bquery%5D=Mr.+Peter,

https://notionpress.com/store/s?NP_Books%5Bquery%5D=P.+Sarkar.

The Following Coupons can be applied on **notionpress.com** till the end of the coupons:

Coupon Codes	Book Name	Buy for	Discount %	Rebate Prices
~~PujaDeal1~~ / ~~Deal1~~	Study of Nouns, Pronouns, Adjectives & Articles (detail study)	~~1~~ & ~~more~~	~~20 & 26~~	~~280~~ ~~224 & 208~~
PujaDeal2 / Deal2	All about Verbs (Forms, Functions, Conjugation, Tense, Voice Change, Forming Questions & Negation)	1 & more	18 & 26	~~420~~ 345 & 311
PujaDeal3 / Deal3	Study of Adverbs, Prepositions, Conjunctions & Interjections	1 & more	20 & 26	~~260~~ 208 & 193
PujaDeal4 / Deal4	Detail Study of Phrases, Clauses & Sentences, including Idioms & Phrasal Verbs	1 & more	20 & 26	~~290~~ 232 & 215
PujaDeal5 / Deal5	Study of Subject-Verb Agreement, Narration Change, Use of Punctuation; including Analysis, Synthesis & Split-up	1 & more	20 & 26	~~301~~ 241 & 223
PujaDeal6 / Deal7	Question Bank of English Grammar & Composition	1 & more	20 & 28	~~559~~ 448 & 403
PujaDeal7 / Deal8/ bulk11	Rhetoric & Prosody	1 & more	20, 26 & 55	~~240~~ 192, 178 &108
PujaDeal8 / Deal9	Steps to Composition (Development of Writing Skill, from Primary to Secondary Level, Part-1)	1 & more	20 & 26	~~300~~ 240 & 222
PujaDeal9 / Deal10	Development of Writing Skill, Part-2	1 & more	18 & 24	~~365~~ 300 & 278
PujaDeal10 / Deal11	Development of Writing Skill, Part-3	1 & more	18 & 24	~~365~~ 300 & 278
unique00 / bulk00	A Book of Advanced Writing Skill, the Complete Version (incl. Part-1, 2 & 3)	1 & more	15 & 23	~~780~~ 663 & 601
unique01 / bulk1/bulk10	Peter's 'English Grammar' (Complete Version of English Grammar)	1 & more	23, 30 & 48	~~1201~~ 925, 841 & 625
unique02/bulk03	English Grammar & Question Bank Together	1 & more	30	~~690~~ 483 & 359
spl01 / bulk04	New English Pal, Class 9 (based on WBBSE syllabus)	1 & more	35 & 47	~~490~~ 319 & 260
spl02 / bulk05	New English Pal, Class 10 (based on WBBSE syllabus)	1 & more	34 & 47	~~480~~ 317 & 255
spl03 / bulk06	New English Pal, Class 5 (based on WBBSE syllabus)	1 & more	29 & 52	~~280~~ 199 & 134
spl04 / bulk07	New English Pal, Class 8 (based on WBBSE syllabus)	1 & more	30 & 46	~~420~~ 294 & 227
spl05 / bulk08	New English Pal, Class 7 (based on WBBSE syllabus)	1 & more	30 & 54	~~400~~ 280 & 184
spl06 / bulk09	New English Pal, Class 6 (based on WBBSE syllabus)	1 & more	30 & 56	~~320~~ 224 & 141
spl07 / bulk12	The Rainbow (A Collection of Short Stories)	1 & more	56 & 56	~~299~~ 132 & 132

Note: For Copies of More Than One, Select The 2nd Coupon Given In Each Row of The First Column